TONIGHT CHARLIE CHAPLIN

GILLIAN PLOWMAN

SERVING THEATRE

S F

SINCE 1830

WWW.SAMUELFRENCH.CO.UK
WWW.SAMUELFRENCH.COM

FOR AMATEUR
PRODUCTION ENQUIRIES

UNITED KINGDOM AND WORLD
EXCLUDING NORTH AMERICA
plays@SamuelFrench-London.co.uk
020 7255 4302/01

UNITED STATES AND CANADA
info@SamuelFrench.com
1-866-598-8449

Each title is subject to availability from Samuel French, depending upon country of performance.

ABOUT THE AUTHOR

Gillian Plowman

Gillian won the Verity Bargate award in 1988 with *Me and My Friend*, a poignantly funny play about the release of four patients from a psychiatric hospital into the community. It was first produced at the Soho Poly Theatre in 1990 and at the Chichester Festival Theatre in 1992, directed by Ian Rickson.

The Purity Game formed part of the opening season of Chichester's Minerva Theatre Studio in 1989. *Storm* was produced in Hastings and London's Soho theatre by Freehand Theatre Company in 2000/01.

Radio plays for the BBC include *The Wooden Pear* in 1991 starring Anna Massey, *Philip and Rowena* in 1993 with Leslie Phillips and Renee Asherson, *A Sea Change* in 1995 with Jenny Funnell and *David's Birthday* in 2000 with Amanda Root and Clare Holman. A film script *Daisyworld* was commissioned by Paramount Pictures.

Boniface and Me, a radio version of *Yours Abundantly from Zimbabwe*, was broadcast in December 2007, the first in a trilogy of radio plays featuring Harriet Walter. *Gracey and Me* was broadcast in 2010 and *Loveness and Me* in 2012.

In 1996, Gillian's play *Padlocked* formed part of the Etcetera Theatre's One-Person Play Festival and *Imagine Imogen* was read at the London New Play Festival in 1997.

Full length plays include *Moments of Glory,* which received a rehearsed reading at the Nuffield Theatre in November 1998, *Another Fine Mess* was toured by the PostScript Theatre Company in 1998/99 and *Pits,* which was a runner up in the 2004 King's Cross Award for new writing.

Yours Abundantly from Zimbabwe, * directed by Annie Castledine, was produced at the Oval House Theatre, London, during Black History Month, October 2008, and *Crooked Wood* was produced at the Jermyn Street Theatre, London, in September 2008.

The End of the Journey, a full-length play, directed by Pamela Howard and linked to the start of World War One was produced in the Pavilion Theatre in Selsey in August 2014, a first production in the near-derelict building for over fifty years. *Tonight in the Pavilion – Charlie Chaplin* was produced there in 2015, and *Tonight in the Pavilion – Laurel and Hardy* in May 2016. These plays prompted the start of the building's renovation as a centre for the arts.

Yours Abundantly from Zimbabwe was featured in *Plays for Today by Women*, published by Aurora Metro Books in 2013 and *Crooked Wood* was published by Oberon Books.

Other plays by Gillian Plowman
published by Samuel French Ltd

Me and My Friend
Beata Beatrix
Cecily
Close to Croydon
David's Birthday
The Janna Years
A Kind of Vesuvius
Philip and Rowena
Two Summers
Umjana Land
There's None So Blind
Tippers
Two Fat Men
Touching Tomorrow
The Allotment
The Window Cleaner

AUTHOR'S NOTE

Charlie Chaplin was the very first icon of the silver screen, and is one of the most recognisable faces in Hollywood, even over a hundred years after the emergence of the Little Tramp. But what of the man behind the moustache? The director holding the camera as well as acting in front of it? The cockney boy beneath the make-up?

Born in London in 1889, his early life was defined by poverty and hardship and in the absence of his father, and with his mother being regularly confined to asylums, he and his brother Sydney spent their childhood in and out of orphanages and workhouses. The workhouse in Kennington is now the Cinema Museum and houses much Chaplin memorabilia.

Charlie survived by making himself invulnerable. 'Even in the orphanage, I thought of myself as the greatest actor in the world. I had to feel the exuberance that comes from utter confidence in myself, without it, you go down to defeat.' This exuberance later became part of his screen persona. The Little Tramp always picks himself up and walks jauntily into the distance.

Chaplin made over eighty films. In 1972 he was honoured with an Academy Award for his 'incalculable effect in making motion pictures the art form of the century'. In 1975 he received a knighthood.

In *Tonight... Charlie Chaplin* it is 1959. Charles Chaplin is seventy years old, talking across the years to the young Charlie Chaplin, the Little Tramp who was never allowed to speak in his films. Now he has a voice.

BIOGRAPHY OF CHARLES CHAPLIN

Early years

Charles Spencer Chaplin was born in London, England, on April 16th 1889. His father was a versatile vocalist and actor; and his mother, known under the stage name of Lily Harley, was an attractive actress and singer, who gained a reputation for her work in the light opera field. Charlie was thrown on his own resources before he reached the age of ten as the early death of his father and the subsequent illness of his mother made it necessary for Charlie and his brother, Sydney, to fend for themselves. Having inherited natural talents from their parents, the youngsters took to the stage as the best opportunity for a career. Charlie made his professional debut as a member of a juvenile group called "The Eight Lancashire Lads" and rapidly won popular favour as an outstanding tap dancer.

Beginning of his career

When he was about fourteen, he got his first chance to act in a legitimate stage show, and appeared as "Billy" the page boy, in support of William Gillette in "Sherlock Holmes". At the close of this engagement, Charlie started a career as a comedian in vaudeville, which eventually took him to the United States in 1910 as a featured player with the Fred Karno Repertoire Company. He scored an immediate hit with American audiences, particularly with his characterization in a sketch entitled "A Night in an English Music Hall". When the Fred Karno troupe returned to the United States in the fall of 1912 for a repeat tour, Chaplin was offered a motion picture contract. He finally agreed to appear before the cameras at the expiration of his vaudeville commitments in November 1913; and his entrance in the cinema world took place that month when he joined Mack Sennett and the Keystone Film Company. His initial salary was $150 a week, but his overnight success on the screen spurred other producers to start negotiations for his services. At the completion of his Sennett contract, Chaplin moved on to the Essanay Company (1915) at a large increase. Sydney Chaplin had then arrived from England, and took his brother's place with Keystone as their leading comedian.

The following year Charlie was even more in demand and signed with the Mutual Film Corporation for a much larger sum to make 12 two-reel comedies. These include *The Floorwalker, The Fireman, The Vagabond, One A.M.* (a production in which he was the only character for the entire two reels with the exception of the entrance of a cab driver in the opening scene), *The Count, The Pawnshop, Behind the Screen, The Rink, Easy Street* (heralded as his greatest production up to that time), *The Cure, The Immigrant* and *The Adventurer.*

Gaining independence

When his contract with Mutual expired in 1917, Chaplin decided to become an independent producer in a desire for more freedom and greater leisure in making his movies. To that end, he busied himself with the construction of his own studios. This plant was situated in the heart of the residential section of Hollywood at La Brea Avenue. Early in 1918, Chaplin entered into an agreement with First National Exhibitors' Circuit, a new organization specially formed to exploit his pictures. His first film under this new deal was *A Dog's Life*. After this production, he turned his attention to a national tour on behalf of the war effort, following which he made a film the US government used to popularize the Liberty Loan drive: *The Bond*. His next commercial venture was the production of a comedy dealing with the war. *Shoulder Arms*, released in 1918 at a most opportune time, proved a veritable mirthquake at the box office and added enormously to Chaplin's popularity. This he followed with *Sunnyside* and *A Day's Pleasure*, both released in 1919.

In April of that year, Chaplin joined with Mary Pickford, Douglas Fairbanks and D.W. Griffith to found the United Artists Corporation. B.B. Hampton, in his "History of the Movies" says: "The corporation was organized as a distributor, each of the artists retaining entire control of his or her respective producing activities, delivering to United Artists the completed pictures for distribution on the same general plan they would have followed with a distributing organization which they did not own. The stock of United Artists was divided equally among the founders. This arrangement introduced a new method into the industry. Heretofore, producers and distributors had been the employers, paying salaries and sometimes a share of the profits to the stars. Under the United Artists system, the stars became their own employers. They had to do their own financing, but they received the producer profits that had formerly gone to their employers and each received his share of the profits of the distributing organization."

The masterpiece features

However, before he could assume his responsibilities with United Artists, Chaplin had to complete his contract with First National. So early in 1921, he came out with a six-reel masterpiece, *The Kid*, in which he introduced to the screen one of the greatest child actors the world has ever known – Jackie Coogan. The next year, he produced "The Idle Class", in which he portrayed a dual character. Then, feeling the need of a complete rest from his motion picture activities, Chaplin sailed for Europe in September 1921. London, Paris, Berlin and other capitals on the continent gave him tumultuous receptions. After an extended vacation, Chaplin returned to Hollywood to resume his picture work and start his active association with United Artists.

Under his arrangement with U.A., Chaplin made eight pictures, each of feature length, in the following order: *A Woman of Paris* (1923) which he wrote, directed and produced, but in which he only appeared in a cameo role and gave the limelight to Edna Purviance and Adolphe Menjou; *The Gold Rush* (1925); *The Circus* (1928); *City Lights* (1931); *Modern Times* (1936); *The Great Dictator* (1940), in which he played a dual role and talked on the screen for the first time; *Monsieur Verdoux* (1947) in which the public saw a new Chaplin, minus his traditional moustache, baggy trousers and wobbly cane; and *Limelight* (1952).

In 1957, he released his comedy *A King in New York* which Chaplin wrote, acted in and directed, as well as composing the music, and in 1966 he produced his last picture *A Countess from Hong Kong* for Universal Pictures, starring Sophia Loren and Marlon Brando.

Chaplin's versatility extended to writing, music and sports. He was the author of at least four books, *My Trip Abroad, A Comedian Sees the World, My Autobiography, My Life in Pictures* as well as all of his scripts. An accomplished musician, though self-taught, he played a variety of instruments with equal skill and facility (playing violin and cello left-handed). He was also a composer, having written and published many songs, among them: *Sing a Song, With You Dear in Bombay,* and *There's Always One You Can't Forget, Smile, Eternally, You are My Song,* as well as the soundtracks for all his films.

Charles Chaplin was one of the rare comedians who not only financed and produced all his films (with the exception of *A Countess from Hong Kong*), but was the author, actor, director and soundtrack composer of them as well.

He died on Christmas day 1977, survived by eight children from his last marriage with Oona O'Neill.

First produced at the Pavilion Theatre, Selsey,
in August 2015 with the following cast:

CHARLIE CHAPLIN . . . . Ryan Moss

CHAPLIN AT 70 . . . . David Flint

HANNAH CHAPLIN . . . . .Josette Coulston

SYDNEY CHAPLIN . . . . Daniel Bowring

MACK SENNETT. . . . . Daniel Bowring

MINNIE CHAPLIN . . . . Briony Laker

HETTY KELLY . . . . Briony Laker

MILDRED HARRIS . . . . Briony Laker

LITA GREY . . . . Briony Laker

JOHN WILLIE JACKSON . . . . David Flint

FRED KARNO . . . . David Flint

DIVORCE LAWYER. . . . . David Flint

DOUGLAS FAIRBANKS. . . . . .Chris Nairne

HARRY WELDON . . . . Michael Gennings

MABEL NORMAND. . . . . Christine Beare

EDNA PURVIANCE. . . . . Christine Beare

MARY PICKFORD. . . . . .Hannah Skelton

PAULETTE GODDARD. . . . . .Hannah Skelton

HENRY LEHRMAN . . . . Colin Martin

AL JOLSON. . . . . .Sam Townsend

BROADWAY BABE AND OPERA SINGER. . . . . Lisa Pow

CROWD AND CHORUS . . . . Members of the cast

PIANIST . . . . Sylvia Rota

DIRECTORS . . . . Pamela Howard, Gillian Plowman

SCENOGRAPHER. . . . . .Pamela Howard

CHOREOGRAPHER . . . . Chris Butler

WARDROBE . . . . Emma Bentley, Georgina Keigher

ASSISTED BY . . . . Sue Graves

PRODUCTION MANAGER. . . . . .Becki Townsend

ASSISTED BY . . . . Charles Townsend, Roland Robinson

BUSINESS MANAGER. . . . . Neil Kimber

LIGHTING . . . . Simon Townsend

SOUND . . . . .Dan Townsend

PRODUCED BY ARTS DREAM SELSEY

Produced at the Cinema Museum, Kennington,
in September 2016 with the following cast:

CHARLIE CHAPLIN . . . . Ryan Moss
CHAPLIN AT 70 . . . . David Flint
HANNAH CHAPLIN . . . . .Josette Coulston
THE YOUNG HANNAH . . . . Lisa Pow
(Lilley Harley)
SYDNEY CHAPLIN . . . . Daniel Bowring
MACK SENNETT. . . . . Daniel Bowring
MINNIE CHAPLIN . . . . Briony Laker
HETTY KELLY . . . . Briony Laker
MILDRED HARRIS . . . . Briony Laker
LITA GREY . . . . Briony Laker
JOHN WILLIE JACKSON . . . . David Flint
FRED KARNO . . . . David Flint
DIVORCE LAWYER. . . . . David Flint
DOUGLAS FAIRBANKS. . . . . .Chris Nairne
HARRY WELDON . . . . Michael Gennings
ORPHANAGE MEN. . . . . Chris Nairne, Michael Gennings
MABEL NORMAND. . . . . Christine Beare
EDNA PURVIANCE. . . . . Christine Beare
MARY PICKFORD . . . . Lisa Pow
PAULETTE GODDARD. . . . . Lisa Pow
MILDRED'S MOTHER . . . . Lisa Pow
HENRY LEHRMAN . . . . Colin Martin
TIMEKEEPER . . . . Colin Martin
AL JOLSON. . . . . .Sam Townsend
BROADWAY BABE. . . . . Lisa Pow
CROWD AND CHORUS . . . . Members of the cast
PIANIST/OPERA SINGER . . . . Sylvia Rota

DIRECTORS . . . . Gillian Plowman, Pamela Howard
MOVEMENT CO-ORDINATOR . . . . Chris Butler
PRODUCTION MANAGER. . . . . .Richard Cooper
LIGHTING DESIGN . . . . Jai Morjaria
ASSOCIATE LIGHTING DESIGNER . . . . Ali Hunter
SOUND DESIGN. . . . . .Chris Drohan
MUSEUM TECHNICIAN. . . . . .David Locke
WARDROBE . . . . Emma Bentley, Georgina Keigher

PRODUCED BY TOBIAS STEED, CAN OF WORMS ENTERPRISES LTD

Dedicated to Jeff Alan

CHARACTER DESCRIPTIONS

CHARLIE CHAPLIN	The Little Tramp. Small, athletic, black curly hair. Plays five to thirty five years. London born.
CHAPLIN AT 70	Smart-suited, urbane. Same height as Charlie. London still in the man.
HANNAH CHAPLIN	Plays twenty to fifty. Beautiful music hall singer, crumbling to premature old age. London born but loves to speak well.
SYDNEY CHAPLIN	Four years older than Charlie. Taller. Plays nine to forty. London born.
MINNIE CHAPLIN	Supportive wife of Sydney, admirer of Charlie. London born and tower of strength. Twenties/thirties.
HETTY KELLY	English fifteen-year-old dancer. Shy. Charlie's first love.
MILDRED HARRIS	Pretty American sixteen-year-old. Charlie's first wife.
LITA GREY	Ambitious sixteen-year-old American actress. Charlie's next wife.
JOHN WILLIE JACKSON	Expansive theatrical entrepreneur, manager of The Eight Lancashire Lads.
FRED KARNO	Middle-aged, ebullient founder of Fred Karno's circus, originally from Devon, widely-travelled.
DIVORCE LAWYER	Middle-aged, American, slick.
DOUGLAS FAIRBANKS	Tall and handsome American film star.
HARRY WELDON	Big, blustery London music hall comedian.
MABEL NORMAND	Vivacious, bossy, young American film star, partner to Mack Sennett. Twenty/thirty.
EDNA PURVIANCE	Intelligent, beautiful American film actress. Twenties/thirties.
MARY PICKFORD	America's sweetheart. Young, pretty, sweet and caring. Curls. Partner of Douglas Fairbanks.
PAULETTE GODDARD	Beautiful, brunette American film star. Twenty two.
HENRY LEHRMAN	Bespectacled brusque American film director.
AL JOLSON	Glamorous and famous /American singer. Thirties.
MUSIC HALL ARTIST	Beautiful female singer of note.
MACK SENNETT	Good-looking successful film producer. Thirties

The original production was titled *Tonight in the Pavilion – Charlie Chaplin*

If you want to use this title, the word Pavilion may be replaced by the name of your own venue

Individual characters and chorus played by a cast of twelve.

CHARLIE CHAPLIN
CHAPLIN aged seventy in 1959
SYDNEY CHAPLIN, Charlie's brother, four years older
HANNAH CHAPLIN, their mother

WOMEN*
HETTY KELLY, aged fifteen, Charlie's first love in old London
MILDRED HARRIS, actress, aged sixteen, Charlie's first wife
LITA GREY, actress, aged sixteen, Charlie's second wife
MINNIE, Sydney's wife
EDNA PURVIANCE, Charlie's great love and leading lady for thirty eight films
MABEL NORMAND, film star
MARY PICKFORD, film star
PAULETTE GODDARD, last leading lady and possible third wife (not ever confirmed)
WOMAN AT PARTY
MILDRED'S MOTHER
BROADWAY BABE and **OPERA SINGER**

MEN*
JOHN WILLIE JACKSON, clog-dancing show Eight Lancashire Lads
FRED KARNO, of circus fame, took Charlie to America
HARRY WELDON, worked for Fred Karno
MACK SENNETT, took Charlie on at Keystone films
DOUGLAS FAIRBANKS, film star
DIVORCE LAWYER, for Mildred Harris
AL JOLSON
MUSIC HALL MC
HENRY LEHRMAN
ORPHANAGE MAN 1
ORPHANAGE MAN 2
OFFICIAL
TIME KEEPER
PIANIST

The props and costume store of the Keystone Film Company, 1915.

There are hidden corners; half-built film sets, hanging sheets. A wardrobe assistant checks a list. A carpenter moves a ladder. From the gloom, and through the clothes rails, a figure emerges. He starts to pick through the rails, finding the trousers, the jacket, the hat, the shoes. He puts them on, practices the walk and, in front of our eyes, the Little Tramp is born.

But we are in 1959. The 70-year-old **CHARLES CHAPLIN** *is present. We shall call him* **CHAPLIN**. *We shall call the Little Tramp,* **CHARLIE.**

CHAPLIN *calls out and catches the tramp's attention.*

Scene 1

CHAPLIN There was a time before that, you know...

CHARLIE What?

CHAPLIN Before the Little Tramp

CHARLIE I know

CHAPLIN Before America, the movies

> **CHARLIE** *does more little tramp moves with his cane and hat.*

> London, Charlie, where you were born. 16th April 1889. Seventy years ago...

CHARLIE You're an old man now

CHAPLIN I am seventy, Charlie but I am not old.

> **CHAPLIN** *spins and turns and does the walk.*

> The time before – 1890s – the great age of the music halls...

Scene 2

The guys and gals throw on boas, hats etc and give a rousing old music hall song – "TA RA! RA! BOOM DE AY!"

CHARLIE *"untramps", is a child.*

MC And now, Ladies and gentlemen, for your delectation, your delight, the purest songstress in town tonight – Miss Lilly Harley!

Lilly Harley was the stage name of **HANNAH CHAPLIN, CHAPLIN'S MOTHER.** *She enters.*

CHARLIE It's our mother! Syd! Syd it's our mother!

SYDNEY *joins him.*

But she's Hannah Chaplin, Syd

SYDNEY That's her stage name – Lilly Harley

CHARLIE I wouldn't do that. I'd always be Charlie Chaplin

SYDNEY Shhh, Charlie, you'll get us thrown out

The two brothers sit, as children.

HANNAH *hugs and kisses them as she goes up to the stage and sings the song.*

"YOU ARE MY HONEYSUCKLE, I AM THE BEE".

To much audience appreciation and the boys' delight.

Until she is afflicted by laryngitis and unable to continue.

The cast becomes the unforgiving audience members and hiss and boo, laughing at her.

HANNAH *is distraught, stumbles and is pulled off by the* **MC.** **CHARLIE** *goes on and sings her song, as a five-year-old. He does well. The "audience" is delighted and coins are thrust into his hands.*

CHARLIE That was her last time on stage. And my first

CHAPLIN *moves to* **CHARLIE** *and they continue the conceit of being able to talk to each other.*

CHAPLIN You were just five years old. Syd, nine...

Scene 3

Their attic room.

SYDNEY What's the matter, Ma?

HANNAH I've got a terrible headache. We'll have to move...can't afford this place...we'll find a nice, cosy room, just the three of us... I've got my sewing machine...there's lots of costumes people need running up for the halls...

(She parodies)

Oh I need feathers from the tip of my head to tip of my...
(she wiggles her backside)

The boys laugh.

And buttons and bows and furbelows

She wiggles and they copy her, laughing.

CHAPLIN *moves.*

CHAPLIN She would sit for hours at a window looking down at the people in the street. It was through watching her that you learned how to study people, how to express emotion with your hands and face

CHARLIE *mimes and postures.*

HANNAH *(doing all the actions)* There comes Bill Smith. He's dragging his feet and his shoes are polished

She does the actions, polishing vigorously.

He looks mad. I'll wager he's had a fight with his wife and come off without his breakfast. Sure enough there he goes into the bakeshop for a bun and coffee!

The boys mime Bill Smith.

The boys laugh.

HANNAH *tries to sing. She can't.*

Their laughter fades.

I lost my voice

CHARLIE We'll find it Ma

They search.

(to **CHAPLIN***)* Lost for all time

CHAPLIN I know. Things went from bad to worse. From three comfortable rooms you moved into two, then one...always hungry...

HANNAH *reels from the pain in her head, collapses and is taken away by two men.*

SYDNEY Where are you taking her?

MAN 1 Lambeth Infirmary, son. And you two are for the workhouse

SYDNEY It's okay Charlie we'll be together...

MAN 2 You – with the big boys. Little'un – with the infants...

They are taken opposite ways.

CHARLIE Sydney! Don't leave me all alone...

Scene 4

In the asylum.

CHAPLIN Poor Hannah. In and out of asylums, her mind faltering, then mending... She retrieved her boys, moving from one back room to another, like a game of draughts, the last move always back to the workhouse before starting again

One time, when she was particularly well, we...they...moved to a room at three Pownall Terrace in the Kennington Road

HANNAH *returns to the attic smiling with a big bag, and the boys run to greet her.*

HANNAH I hope you've remembered your manners and your good talking!

CHAPLIN Sheep were driven daily past Pownall Terrace on their way to a nearby slaughterhouse. One of them escaped running pell-mell among the crowds in the street

The boys are killing themselves laughing, watching the chaos.

SYDNEY They've caught it!

CHARLIE Caught it!

They cheer.

SYDNEY Off to the slaughterhouse

CHARLIE *(realising, weeping, running to* **HANNAH***)* They're going to kill it! They're going to kill it...

She hugs him.

HANNAH You see how it is, Charlie. Laughter and sorrow go hand in hand

CHAPLIN The tragic and the comic. Those words of my mother's... I hear them as clear now as I did all those years ago. All my films came from those words of my mother's

HANNAH Come on, boys...look what I've got

SYDNEY Where'd you get them?

HANNAH There they were, lying on the cobbles, waiting for cockney feet...oh la

She is a little strange and they look at each other.

She gets clogs out of her bag and they dance the clogs.

Enter **JOHN WILLIE JACKSON**.

JWJ Well now, well now you, young fella me lad, you heard of the Eight Lancashire Lads? The clog-dancing troupe. John Willie Jackson at your command...

HANNAH Eight Lancashire Lads?

JWJ Well I've only got seven as one of 'em's deserted, and all me posters say eight. Hundreds of posters I've got. Don't want to waste 'em so I need another lad

HANNAH They're cockney lads. Nicely spoken mind

JWJ Your lad here will be just fine – after intense rehearsing you understand. Music halls all round the country, full board and lodging and half a crown wages paid direct to you, ma'am

HANNAH What about Sydney?

SYDNEY I'm going to be an actor, Ma. Going round all the theatrical agencies. Going to follow in your footsteps, and father's

HANNAH He could sing a song on a stage all right, but he drank himself to death, Sydney. *(She raises her finger to both of them)* Lay off the booze, and watch how you talk. Doesn't matter where you come from...

The Lancashire Lads enter and clog dance to music. (Costume of blouse, knickerbockers, lace collar and red clogs.)

Scene 5

CHAPLIN Even to a ten-year-old in a troupe of clog dancers, the music halls of those times provided an incomparable schooling in method, technique and discipline. A music hall act had to seize and hold its audience, make its mark within a very limited time – five minutes…the audience was not indulgent and the competition was relentless – Sarah Bernhardt might find herself following Lockhart's elephants on the bill. You had to learn the secrets of attack and structure, the need to give the act a crescendo – a beginning, a middle, and a smashing exit – to grab the applause. You had to command every sort of audience from a lethargic Monday first house to the Saturday rowdies

Fred Karno of course was the king of music hall knockabout comedy

KARNO Custard pies and buckets of whitewash, trick cyclists and spinning plates, high wires and wooden stilts, spinning clubs and fire torches are always on the bill. Drunks

He points at them and they do drunks.

I've got twenty troupes touring all over England and America. I can spot a good 'un a mile off. How much am I paying you?

SYDNEY Four pounds a week

My brother Charlie has been on the halls since he was this high. I need a plumber's helper in my sketch – you know where he knocks the nail through a wall into a water pipe?

KARNO Where's the other one gone?

SYDNEY Gone

KARNO Gone! When anyone leaves this company, it's like taking a screw out of a very delicate piece of machinery. You do not be *gone!*

SYDNEY He's gone. See Charlie, Mr Karno

KARNO *sees* **CHARLIE**.

You look undernourished. How old are you?

CHARLIE Seventeen

KARNO Never

CHARLIE It's a question of make-up, Mr Karno

Circus scene with as many acts as possible ensues.

KARNO All right. I'm from humble beginnings meself. Give you a trial, on account of Syd here. I want comedy – that comes from–

SYDNEY Perfect timing

KARNO And the unexpected. Keep it wistful. When you knock a man down, kiss him on the head. If you hit someone hard, just look sorry for a few minutes. That makes the action funnier. You can come on with Harry Weldon in The Football Match. You enter as the villain to bribe Harry, the star goalkeeper, into throwing the game...

HARRY WELDON All those ruddy extra rehearsals cos of this new fella

KARNO The golf will have to wait, Harry

HARRY WELDON *shakes his head crossly.*

SYDNEY Touchy is Harry. Top of the bill and jealous of anybody new who might want to topple him

CHARLIE I don't want to topple him, just learn...

Sketch. The actors becoming audience.

CHARLIE *enters threateningly, his back to the audience.* **CHARLIE** *has reddened his nose and stuck a moustache on. He turns with great unction, his nose dominating. Gusts of laughter from the audience. He does a comedy routine. He loses a button and his pants fall down.*

Audience is ribald.

Looking for the button, he picks something up and throws it away with a grimace.

Confounded rabbits

Audience roars.

WELDON *waiting to come on can't understand the laughter.*
CHARLIE *is supposed to feed him, the principal comedian.*
He comes on to re-establish dominance and **CHARLIE** *grabs him ad-libbing.*

Quick! I'm undone! A pin!

More laughter.

HARRY WELDON *and* **CHARLIE** *with* **KARNO.**

HARRY WELDON We didn't rehearse any of that. What the devil's going on?

KARNO He made them laugh

CHARLIE He's jealous

HARRY WELDON I have more talent in my arse than you have in your whole body!

CHARLIE That's where your talent lies!

Exit **HARRY WELDON.**

CHAPLIN You had a big mouth Charlie

CHARLIE And you never let me speak! The Little Tramp was silent all his life

CHAPLIN No, you spoke the truth. In the human heart, for some reason or other, there is love of truth. Even in slapstick comedy, it is the truth of the situation that makes people laugh. The whole world understands when they watch your face, look into your eyes, see your grin. They understand that in China and Ceylon. Everywhere in the world, they see the truth that words would destroy...

Scene 6

CHARLIE *and* SYDNEY *go to see* HANNAH. *She is in the asylum.*

SYDNEY Charlie and I are sharing a bill together

HANNAH Don't fall in the river, son

SYDNEY What?

HANNAH The river Jordan

CHARLIE Living together now in Brixton

HANNAH They won't let me out of here. The river's too deep. No! No! Don't cross

They turn to leave.

If you'd made that cup of tea for me, Charlie, it would have all been different

They leave her.

CHARLIE What cup of tea?

SYDNEY We couldn't look after her, Charlie...

CHARLIE But...

SYDNEY She's ill

CHAPLIN *(to us)* What cup of tea?

Scene 7

A girl is dancing. The melancholy CHARLIE *has fallen for the fifteen-year-old* HETTY KELLY.

CHARLIE Hetty Kelly, you are the most beautiful dancer in the whole of London

HETTY I'm... I'm training you know. I'm not a dancer yet

CHARLIE Can I walk you home? Can I meet you tomorrow? Will you meet me on Sunday?

HETTY I...yes

They walk. He makes her laugh with his mimed antics.

CHARLIE How much do you love me?

HETTY I'm too young for love

CHARLIE No you're not

HETTY Fifteen

CHARLIE I love you

HETTY My mother says...

CHARLIE Do you love me?

HETTY I...

CHARLIE Mothers can make you sad

HETTY She says that I ...that we...

CHARLIE You see

HETTY That you should stop...seeing me

CHARLIE I love you...you are my honeysuckle

HETTY I don't know if we're in love

CHARLIE I do

HETTY Please...

Suddenly.

CHARLIE We must part and never see each other again?

She doesn't know what else to say.

HETTY Yes

She goes, touching **CHAPLIN** *briefly on her way.*

CHAPLIN You loved and lost

CHARLIE *(whispers)* My first love. Sometimes I think I look for her in every girl I meet

But I had my violin...

CHARLIE *always has his violin.*

Scene 8

The guys and gals embark for America, singing a riff:

All aboard the SS Cairnrona to cross the Atlantic. We're taking A Night in an English Music Hall all around America – Winnipeg and Chicago, Portland and San Francisco, Cleveland and Kansas City

CHAPLIN *(to* **CHARLIE***)* 1910. You're twenty one now

KARNO Old enough and big enough and clever enough for anything!

CHAPLIN And from coast to coast, the Inebriated Swell had them laughing in the aisles of America

> **CHARLIE** *dons the askew winged collar and red cheeks of the inebriate.*

CHARLIE *(to* **CHAPLIN***)* I loved America. When the tour ended in 1912 and I came back to England, Syd had married and I had no home. After the United States, England seemed small and tight and dismal. I was happy when Karno sent me back for a second tour

CHAPLIN Top billing

CHARLIE Yes

> *He starts to perform the drunk.*

CHAPLIN Unanimously praised by the press

CHARLIE Yes

> *Continues performing.*

CHAPLIN And seen in New York by Mack Sennett. With the creation of the Keystone Cops in 1912 he might well be said to have created American comedy. And he wanted you...

CHARLIE From Karno to Keystone! My final performance on stage was at Kansas City on 28 November 1913

The cast gather round him, the inebriate, drinks in hand.
Goodbyes and handshakes and **CHARLIE,** *trembling, turning*
from them with tears in his eyes, stumbling away.

CHAPLIN Film was the coming thing. With the advent of small
storefront theatres, known as nickelodeons, motion pictures
of ten or so minutes were becoming increasingly popular.
The poor and the illiterate flocked to these silent shows, to be
seen at the price of a nickel. For immigrants, who could not
yet read English, they provided immediate access to American
life. They offered what seemed at the time to be spellbinding
realism except that the actors moved faster than real life. They
sat on wooden seats and brought their own refreshments with
them. Sometimes the screen was little more than a bed sheet
against the back wall

CHARLIE *arrives at Keystone. People are everywhere – in costume,*
make-up. Beautiful girls. **MABEL NORMAND** *is banging on a*
prop door, shouting Let me in! Let me in!

He is overwhelmed, turns away.

Go on *(urging him)* There's Sennett now

MACK SENNETT Mister Chaplin! Charles Chaplin?

CHARLIE Yes

MACK Mack Sennett

CHARLIE Mister Sennett

MACK You look younger than you did on stage

CHARLIE I'm an actor

MACK Mabel!

She joins them. They are obviously an item.

Mabel Normand. See how young the old drunk is

MABEL I like your work

CHARLIE You seen much of it?

MABEL One show – in New York. Very slick

CHARLIE Fred Karno is a perfectionist

MABEL Mack Sennett is a perfectionist

MACK Can you fall off a ladder?

CHARLIE Can I...?

MACK I mean, can you do a funny sprawl off a step-ladder without breaking your bones?

CHARLIE *does this.*

CHARLIE Yes. What's the scenario?

MACK We have no scenario. We get an idea then follow the natural sequence of events until it leads up to a chase, which is the essence of our comedy

CHARLIE What do you want me to do?

MACK Make a movie. My top director, Mr Henry Lehrman, wants you to play a dude in his new film about a newspaper reporter

He points out **LEHRMAN**. *He and* **CHARLIE** *don't take to each other.*

CHARLIE We had no story. I could see Lehrman was groping for ideas. I had plenty. I crammed in every conceivable gag. I suggested business for others in the cast...

He deliberately cut it all out. Why would he do that?

CHAPLIN Seems he thought you were a bit of a know-all. Couldn't keep your mouth shut

CHARLIE I was trying to make it better

CHAPLIN An inexperienced, stiff little newcomer...telling Lehrman his job?

CHARLIE I don't think he knows his job. It's all mechanical with him. Doesn't he realize that film is about the truth?

CHAPLIN Hah! Who told you that!

CHARLIE You know how Henry Lehrman will go down in history? The man who directed Charlie Chaplin in his first film. Badly

MACK I don't like it Mabel. I think I've hooked myself a dead one here. He's not funny

MABEL I understand the funny bits are on the cutting room floor. I want to work with Charlie, Mack – I've got a feeling about this...

MACK We need some gags here. *(To* **CHARLIE***)* Put on comedy make-up! Anything will do

CHAPLIN This is where we came in!

CHARLIE I have no idea what to put on

CHAPLIN Make everything a contradiction

> **CHARLIE LOOKS AT CHAPLIN.** *He finds the clothes again and dresses as he talks.*

CHARLIE Baggy pants – I think these must be Fatty Arbuckle's. Everything a contradiction. Tight coat. The hat small – a bowler hat. The shoes large

He puts them on.

CHAPLIN I first thought of you in terms of satire. Your indescribable trousers represented in my mind a revolt from convention, your moustache the vanity of man, your hat and your cane attempts to be dignified and your shoes the impediments that were always in your way

CHARLIE Might have to wear the shoes on the wrong feet to keep 'em on

CHAPLIN But you persisted in growing more and more human and getting nearer to the heart of the matter

CHARLIE Should I look young or old?

CHAPLIN Sennett expected an older man remember?

CHARLIE A small moustache. It will add age without hiding my expression

CHAPLIN And the walk?

CHARLIE You remember that old rum soak, Rummy Binks – I remember him when I was a kid – used to hold the horses for coachmen when they popped in for a quick drink at the Queen's Head on the Lambeth Walk

CHAPLIN Large, misshapen old feet. Shuffled as he walked the horses to the trough

CHARLIE That's Rummy

They do the walk together and then **CHARLIE** *goes swinging off with his cane to confront* **MACK** *and* **MABEL**.

CHAPLIN *(to audience)* Those coachmen would throw Rummy a coin or two, and that's how he earned his living. Died in poverty. And the walk we stole from him made Charles Chaplin one of the richest men in the world. Tell me, where's the justice in that

CHARLIE *(to* **MACK**) This fellow is many-sided you know – a tramp, a gentleman, a poet, a dreamer, a lonely fellow always hopeful of romance and adventure, he would have you believe he is a scientist, a musician, a duke, a polo player...however he is not above picking up cigarette butts or robbing a baby of his candy. And of course if the occasion warrants it, he will kick a lady in the rear, but only in extreme anger

He kicks **MABEL** *in the rear and she reacts dramatically in character.* **MACK SENNETT** *roars with laughter.*

MACK All right. Get on the set and see what you can do there

CHARLIE With Lehrman?

MACK Yes!

CHARLIE is unhappy.

MABEL And me, Charlie. My new film – Mabel's Strange Predicament

She demonstrates a bit of **MABEL**.

CHARLIE He cuts out all the funny bits

MACK I'll be the judge of that

An excerpt from Mabel's Strange Predicament *may be shown here.*

CHARLIE Mabel's Strange Predicament – the first film in which the Little Tramp appeared

CHAPLIN Not the first released

MACK *(to* CHARLIE*)* Wear that! Take Lehrman and a camera and get down to the Kids Auto Races at Venice Beach!

CHAPLIN Hard to believe there was a world before Charlie Chaplin.

An excerpt from Kid Auto Races at Venice *can be shown behind them as they talk.*

Suddenly out of the crowd...he steps

CHARLIE It was nothing. A Lehrman one joke. He was trying to shoot the race and this silly little man was spoiling it. It was rubbish. That wasn't the Tramp

He grabs MABEL*'s hand.*

This is where he appears for the first time. With Mabel...

CHARLIE *and* MABEL *re-enact a bit.*

CHAPLIN *Kid Auto Races* came out on 7th February 1914. *Mabel's Strange Predicament* was released two days later...

CHARLIE Look at me! This is me! I don't know where you are now. Who you are now? So far away. So un...knowing... But in that film with Mabel...the moment I was dressed, the clothes and the make-up, I started to feel, to know who I am. The moment I strutted on to that set, gags and ideas raced through my mind...and I came full-blown into the world

MABEL Charlie, that Little Tramp fellow. Has he got a great future!

(She exits delightedly shouting) Mack! Mack!

CHAPLIN By 1915 you were the most famous man in the world.

What if, a century later, they're still laughing at those Keystone comedies

CHARLIE No...

CHAPLIN But what if...you're making something now that is so remarkable that it will last a hundred years?

CHARLIE Then I have only one thing to say to those people in a hundred years time: a day without laughter is a day wasted

Scene 9

SYDNEY *enters reading a letter.*

SYDNEY Sunday 9th August 1914

Yes it really is your brother after all these years. Well, Syd, I have made good. All the theatres feature my name in big letters – Charlie Chaplin here today. I tell you in this country I am a big box office attraction. All the managers tell me that I have fifty letters a week from men and women from all parts of the world. It is wonderful how popular I am in such a short time and next year I hope to make a bunch of dough...

Mr Sennett is in New York. He said he would write to you and make you an offer. I told him you would do great in pictures. He said he would give you one hundred and fifty dollars a week to start with but I said you were getting that now! *(SYDNEY laughs)* Don't come for less than one hundred and seventy-five, understand?

Now about that money for Mother – do you think it is safe to send it while the war is on, or do you think it better for you to pay my share and we will arrange things later? I hope they don't make you fight over there. This war is terrible. Love to Minnie. Your loving brother... *(Move into next scene)*

Scene 10

...Charlie

SYDNEY *and* **MINNIE** *with suitcases.*

SYDNEY Charlie!

MINNIE *sits on her case.*

Can you put me up for the night?

CHARLIE Certainly not. I don't know you

SYDNEY Don't you remember Archibald?

CHARLIE Why it's the captain, my dear old captain. Why I haven't seen you since we were in the army together

SYDNEY Do you remember when we were in the Sudan surrounded by the enemy on every side? There we stood with our retreat cut off

CHARLIE With our what cut off?

SYDNEY Our retreat cut off

CHARLIE Three days and nights without water. Not a drain of water but what did we do?

SYDNEY Drank it neat!

CHARLIE Well how's the world been using you?

SYDNEY Now and then

CHARLIE Where are you working?

SYDNEY Here and there

CHARLIE What do you work at?

SYDNEY This and that

CHARLIE Do you have to work hard?

SYDNEY On and off

CHARLIE Are you looking for a job?

SYDNEY Yes and no

CHARLIE Well you don't look half as smart as you used to

They sing and dance When Father Papered The Parlour.

SYDNEY I was too old for the draft

CHARLIE They're saying I'm a slacker. Saying I should be over there fighting this war

SYDNEY Who's saying?

CHARLIE Newspapers

SYDNEY Take no notice Charlie. You're contributing to the war by keeping people's chins up. They go to the pictures and you make 'em laugh. They're even setting up projectors in hospitals, so's the men can watch Charlie Chaplin films

CHARLIE I've sent one hundred and fifty thousand pounds to the war fund Syd

SYDNEY Blimey Charlie

CHARLIE I went to the recruiting office to register – turned down as I was underweight

SYDNEY Well then

CHARLIE And you know Douglas Fairbanks and Mary Pickford...?

SYDNEY The king and queen of Hollywood!

Scene Out

DOUGLAS FAIRBANKS *and* MARY PICKFORD *arrive, very glamorous, to much applause by adoring public.*

CHARLIE We're touring the country to rally support for Liberty bonds – for the American war effort

They proclaim.

DOUGLAS The Germans are at your door! We've got to stop them! And we will stop them if you buy Liberty bonds

MARY Remember, each bond you buy will save a soldier's life – a mother's son! and will bring this war to an early victory

CHARLIE You people out there. I want you to forget all about percentages in this Liberty loan. Human life is at stake and no-one ought to worry about what rate of interest the bonds are going to bring or what he can make by purchasing them.

DOUGLAS Money is needed. Money to support the great army and navy of Uncle Sam

MARY This very minute the Germans occupy a position of advantage, and we have to get the dollars

CHARLIE Buy Liberty bonds and we can drive that old devil, the Kaiser, out of France!

Adoring public rush to shake them by the hand. A woman hugs MARY.

Scene Back In

SYDNEY You couldn't do more than that Charlie

CHAPLIN *(to audience)* For years afterwards I continued to receive white feathers and anonymous letters for my failure to fight. It haunted me...

MINNIE You not married Charlie?

CHARLIE Trouble is Minnie, there are women everywhere in this film business, and they're all trouble. Not like you

He kisses her.

MINNIE What sort of trouble?

CHARLIE I told Sennett I wanted to write and direct my own comedies but he wouldn't hear of it and assigned me to Mabel Normand...

MINNIE *Mabel Normand...?* Charlie...you know *everybody*

CHARLIE ...who had just started directing her own pictures, which nettled me because, because charming as she is, she doesn't understand comedy

In one scene she wanted me to stand with a hose and water down the road so that the villain's car would skid on it. I suggested standing on the hose so that the water can't come out and when I look down the nozzle I unconsciously step off the hose and the water squirts in my face. But she shut me up quickly

MABEL *There's no time for that. Do what you're told*

CHARLIE I'm sorry, Miss Normand, I will not do what I'm told. I don't think you're competent to tell me what to do

MACK *What the hell's the idea?*

CHARLIE The story needs gagging up but she won't listen to any of my suggestions

MACK *You'll do what you're told or get out, contract or no contract*

CHARLIE If I'm fired, well I'm fired. But I'm conscientious and just as keen to make a good picture as you are

SYDNEY Are you fired?

CHARLIE Hah! The next morning Mack received a telegram from the New York office telling him to hurry up with more Chaplin films, as there was a terrific demand for them!

SYDNEY I always knew you would make good

CHARLIE I've learnt a lot at Keystone, Syd, but from now on I will write my own parts

CHAPLIN You never learned how to say goodbye well. Walked out of Keystone one Saturday night and began at Essanay in Chicago on Monday morning

Scene 11

CHAPLIN It was disturbing moving from one studio to another. You had to organize another working unit, a cameraman, an assistant director and a stock company

CHARLIE I need to find a new leading lady

SYDNEY There's a girl who goes to Tate's café. Edna Purviance. They say she's very pretty

CHARLIE *finds* **EDNA PURVIANCE** *in the café.*

EDNA I'm not an actress. I've just taken a business course

CHARLIE But still...

(*To* **CHAPLIN**) A bit sad. Just finished a love affair. I thought... well, at least she would be decorative to my comedies even if she can't act or has any humour

And takes her to a party – large group talking and drinking – him boasting.

Scene 12

CHARLIE I could hypnotise anyone in the room

EDNA What nonsense. No one could hypnotise me

CHARLIE You are the perfect subject. I bet you ten dollars that I'll put you to sleep in sixty seconds

EDNA All right, I'll bet

CHARLIE Now if you're not well afterwards, don't blame me for it. Of course it will be nothing serious.

A WOMAN You're very foolish.

EDNA The bet still goes. Sixty seconds

TIMEKEEPER Go

> **CHARLIE** *makes dramatic gestures.*

CHARLIE In sixty seconds you will be completely unconscious

> *Goes near her face. Whispers.*

Fake it!

> **EDNA** *staggers, falls into* **CHARLIE'***s arms.*

Help me put her on the couch

> **EDNA** *recovers, looking bewildered and everyone cheers.*

> **CHARLIE** *and* **CHAPLIN** *look at each other and grin.*

EDNA *(to* **CHAPLIN***)* Eight years

CHAPLIN Yes

EDNA Thirty-five films in eight years

CHAPLIN You were his incomparable leading lady

EDNA I loved him, you know

CHAPLIN He loved you

EDNA I fell in love with him in The Tramp

The goodbye scene from the film may be shown, then the final one when **CHARLIE** *walks away.*

If the film clip is not shown, use the following speech:

EDNA *That final scene, when he's walking away into the distance, all alone... I wanted to call him back*

I wanted to call him back

CHAPLIN And ruin his exit?

CHARLIE I took that risk, you know

CHAPLIN What?

CHARLIE Discarding comedy for pathos. Essanay were horrified

CHAPLIN You walk dejectedly away from the camera, but happiness breaks through. The little dance upon the road is a form of self-definition. You are free. You will never be truly alone because you are infinitely resourceful. You have the will to live in a world that may not be worth living in. You are everyman, Charlie. If you can survive, so can they. That's why the world loves you

CHARLIE *cocks a snook at* **CHAPLIN**.

CHARLIE You wouldn't let me talk, but you couldn't stop me cocking a snook or kicking some official in the arse. Take *The Immigrant*

Everyone rocks as though on a stormy boat. An excerpt from The Immigrant *showing the immigrants on the boat may be shown as* **CHARLIE** *talks.*

All those people, like me, arriving in a foreign land, the land of promise, and just as the Statue of Liberty comes in sight with those words carved into it...

CHAPLIN *Give me your tired, your poor, your huddled masses yearning to breathe free, the wretched refuse of your teeming shore*

CHARLIE ...we are roped off! What liberty eh? What did they say about that?

CHAPLIN They didn't complain at the time. It was later. Much later. After your time

Out of scene

OFFICIAL Mr Chaplin, why did you never become an American citizen?

CHAPLIN Because I am an Englishman

Back in scene

They threw me out of America, Charlie

The final scene of The Immigrant *when* **CHARLIE** *takes* **EDNA** *to the registry office in the pouring rain may be shown.*

If the clip is not shown, the following speech should be added:

CHAPLIN *in the pouring rain, the two immigrants who fell in love on the boat go to the register office to be married.*

EDNA Can they build a life together in an alien world?

CHAPLIN Mmm

EDNA We should have married...

CHAPLIN *nods.*

But

CHAPLIN I know

EDNA She was so young. Mildred Harris...

Scene 13

CHARLIE *is entranced by the sixteen-year-old* MILDRED HARRIS. *Has fallen for her, makes her laugh, embraces her. There is* MILDRED'*s* MOTHER... *always there.*

CHAPLIN Charlie... Charlie...she's sixteen. You're twenty nine!

CHARLIE Seventeen

CHAPLIN It's Hetty Kelly, isn't it? You can't forget her

CHARLIE Did you ever forget her?

CHAPLIN No...but that was then. Now you have Edna

CHARLIE Mildred's a pretty girl. All I need to make a comedy – a park, a policeman and a pretty girl

CHAPLIN Then leave it at that. Make your comedy. Don't romance this young girl

CHARLIE *cocks a snook at* CHAPLIN *and turns back to kiss* MILDRED.

EDNA *watches and walks away.*

MILDRED Charlie, I'm pregnant

CHARLIE *looks at her, at her* MOTHER, *at* CHAPLIN.

CHAPLIN I married Mildred. Of course. It turned out she wasn't pregnant. We tried to make a go of it and when she really did become pregnant, I was a happy man. Norman Spencer Chaplin was born on the 7th July 1919. My son, my firstborn... three days later, he died

CHARLIE *holds the dead baby and cries and cries.* MILDRED *stands close by but neither can console the other.*

On his gravestone was carved the words The Little Mouse.

Scene 14

CHARLIE Edna – we're going to a show!

CHARLIE *goes one way to watch a vaudeville act with* **EDNA**. **MILDRED** *goes to the divorce court.*

Vaudeville Act – **BROADWAY BABE** *and the chorus sing* *"HOW YA GONNA KEEP 'EM DOWN ON THE FARM".*

SYDNEY First National are offering a one hundred and twenty-five thousand dollar advance on each film and a direct split of the profits

MINNIE What's your next comedy, Charlie?

CHARLIE Norman Spencer Chaplin is lost but in my imagination he is here... I can restore him to life...

He turns to **EDNA**.

You play an unwed mother who is discharged from the charity hospital with the infant in your arms. You are heart riven. You find a parked limousine and put the baby inside with a note asking him to be loved and cared for

EDNA *begins to act this out with a scarf as the baby.*

The car is stolen and the thieves abandon the baby. And I find him...

Out of scene

Divorce court.

LAWYER What did he say or do with reference to your friends if he should find them in his house

MILDRED He was not nice to them. He wouldn't come home if I had them

LAWYER How often did that occur, Mrs Chaplin?

MILDRED All the time. He would never tell me when he would be home; he said he had to be free to live his own life and do as he pleased

LAWYER Did he give you any reason why he stayed away?

MILDRED He said I had disgraced him by going out

LAWYER Tell the court what happened at that time

MILDRED I cried and begged him to come back home and I fainted and he said that I was acting silly and he didn't see why he should come back

LAWYER Was his method of talking to you kindly or otherwise

MILDRED Not kindly. He said that he knew he did not want to live with me any more; that he had tried to change me and he saw that it was impossible and that I wasn't any good and that he couldn't trust me

She turns to CHAPLIN.

All I wanted was enough money to look after my mother

Back in the Scene

CHAPLIN When you found the abandoned baby, you took him home to your little room at the top of a lodging house

CHARLIE The first time you let me have a home...be inside

CHAPLIN And the room...it was...

CHARLIE Just like the one we shared with mother in Pownall Terrace – narrow bed, a table and some old chairs, bare boards on the floor and the paper peeling off the walls...you made me relive it all...raise a baby till he's five years old... I loved making *The Kid*. I loved that little boy

CHAPLIN I know

CHARLIE Like I would have loved...my son...

CHAPLIN I know...

An excerpt from The Kid *may be shown but only if licensed by the* **CHAPLIN** *office**.

Scene 15

HANNAH *appears with* **SYD** *and* **MINNIE**.

SYDNEY Charlie!

CHARLIE So...you've come to live in America now

HANNAH Look at your suit! It's a disgrace, Charlie. It's a good job I have arrived – get you sorted out, m'lad

SYDNEY That's Charlie's famous Little Fellow, Ma. He's so famous that they want him to appear everywhere, but he can't be everywhere, Ma, so there's lots of pretend Charlies, going to all these places to keep the people happy

Lots of **CHARLIE CHAPLINS** *appear. They do the* **CHARLIE CHAPLIN** *dance.*

Come on Ma. I'll make you that cup of tea...

CHAPLIN You're like her, Charlie. The eyes, the smile, the gestures of the hands...

Scene 16

DOUGLAS FAIRBANKS *and* **MARY PICKFORD** *appear and they and* **CHARLIE** *raise glasses.*

DOUGLAS We have had enough of studios dictating salaries and schedules. It will be more profitable to invest our own money, produce our own films and distribute the finished product ourselves

MARY Here's to United Artists – Douglas Fairbanks, Mary Pickford, Charlie Chaplin

DOUGLAS Your next film – for United Artists, Charlie? It must be an epic. The greatest!

CHAPLIN I picked up a book on the plight of some immigrants to America in the middle of the nineteenth century. They had found themselves stranded in the snowbound wastes of the Sierra Nevada where, in conditions of famine and death, the survivors resorted to eating dogs and saddles, as well as their own boots, to stay alive. So the germ of *The Gold Rush* was planted

CHARLIE I have to find a new heroine. Edna is just not suitable for this role. She is getting a little heavy...

CHAPLIN You have your eye on someone?

CHARLIE Lita Grey

> **LITA** *is a laughing pretty sixteen-year-old.*

CHAPLIN No Charlie. Don't do the same thing again. This is not a park a policeman and a pretty girl

CHARLIE She's a good actress

CHAPLIN Another sixteen-year-old!

CHARLIE Don't you put that on me! As if it was nothing to do with you! Youth and beauty makes the girl. And it passes like spring into summer and winter, and spring must come again! You. You dictated that Charlie must have a girl to fall in love with, to entrance the public and make the comedy and the pathos. You...

CHAPLIN ...should not have taken her to bed!

CHARLIE Oh. You know that now.

CHAPLIN *(to us)* The set of a mining camp was built and a pass through the snow created by professional ski jumpers who carved steps out of the frozen snow on the side of Mount Lincoln. Five hundred derelicts from Sacramento were brought by train and in single file they climbed the slope of the frozen waste

Excerpt from The Gold Rush – *the first scene – may be shown but only if licensed by the* **CHAPLIN** *office*.*

CHARLIE Cooking my boot and eating it as though it were a rare delicacy at the The Ritz... I thought the hunger of my childhood comes back to me, and becomes the spring of comedy

The scene in which **CHARLIE** *cooks a boot then eats it can be shown but only if licensed by the* **CHAPLIN** *office*.*

The darned boot was made of liquorice – you made us do so many takes with so many different boots – we were violently ill for days!

CHAPLIN And so you dreamed of dinner parties, and bread rolls

CHARLIE *re-enacts part of the Bread Roll sequence from* The Gold Rush.

Interrupted by.

LITA I'm pregnant Charlie

CHARLIE Then I have to find another leading lady

A dignified **LITA** *is desolate.*

CHAPLIN *(to audience)* He found Georgia Hale. And he married Lita. *The Gold Rush* took seventeen months to complete. At a cost of one million dollars, it was the most expensive comedy of the silent era, but with earnings of six million dollars, it was eventually the most successful

DOUGLAS What does it feel like to be a millionaire, Charlie?

CHARLIE   Nothing fails like success. Money never satisfied a spiritual or intellectual need. I doubt if a rich man ever has a real friend...

DOUGLAS   Hey, you're surrounded by friends!

MARY   What do you mean, Charlie?

CHARLIE   A part of my childhood was spent in a London workhouse. When Christmas time came round a big table was spread and on it were laid little presents – tin watches, bags of candy, picture books...

I was seven years old. We all formed in a line and long before it was my turn to reach the table and select what I wanted I had picked out with my eye a big, fat red apple for my present. It was the biggest apple I had ever seen outside a picture book. My eye and stomach got bigger and bigger as I approached that apple. But when I was about fifth from the table, somebody in authority pushed me out of line and took me back to my room. No Christmas present for you this year, Charlie. You keep the other boys awake by telling stories...

The still of the Little Tramp in the snowbound cabin, shivering and hungry, looking directly at the camera fills the screen.

CHAPLIN   The image of the Little Tramp is now fixed forever in the public imagination. His yearnings are as palpable as his bowler hat and cane; he needs food, money and love in that order. His fate is as inseparable from that of any common man

CHARLIE   I was always impoverished, while you became a millionaire

CHAPLIN   What I gave you, my little fellow, was an unbreakable strength of spirit. And, believe me, I never forgot poverty

CHARLIE   I had to marry Lita, Syd. She was pregnant, too young – they were gunning for me. But it's no good – we can't make it work

SYDNEY   You can't you mean. She's in love with you Charlie. She loves you

CHARLIE   She's not the one

SYDNEY   Then who is?

CHARLIE I don't know, Sydney. My work is my life. I can't do marriage

SYDNEY She's given you two fine sons in two years – Minnie adores little Charlie Chaplin junior and the babe's a cracker

CHARLIE Sydney. He's called Sydney. There's a new Charlie and Sydney, Syd

SYDNEY You've got to give him a better life than we had

CHARLIE They won't want for anything. Lita will have plenty of money to raise them

SYDNEY What was it you said – money never satisfied a spiritual need? What about a father's love, Charlie

CHARLIE *nods. He knows.*

You know Minnie can't have children, don't you Charlie...

CHARLIE *looks after him as he walks away.* **DOUGLAS** *swashbuckles in!*

Scene 17

DOUGLAS Charlie! Warner Brothers have made a talking picture – *The Jazz Singer*. Al Jolson is speaking! Singing a song – My Mammy! People can not only see him, they can hear him! They can hear him, Charlie!

Chorus and **AL JOLSON** *sing* "*MY MAMMY*".

United Artists will make talking pictures. This is 1927 and the talkies are the future. We've got a wireless broadcast lined up so that audiences can hear our voices...

CHARLIE *(to* **CHAPLIN***)* But you wouldn't let me, would you. You would never let me speak

CHAPLIN How can you speak? What kind of voice can you be given? You are Everyman, a symbol of the human world. If you speak English, it would affect your reception by foreign audiences who would no longer have the direct contact with the Little Tramp. The Chinese, Japanese, the Hindu, the Hottentot all understand you. What voice, what words could match that exquisite, sublimely graceful little fellow. You are a child of the silences

DOUGLAS We can't be left behind, Charlie. You must make your next film a talkie

CHARLIE Yes!

CHAPLIN But I couldn't let you speak – The Tramp, in City Lights – who fell in love with the beautiful blind flower girl, who thought he was a millionaire. The closing scene...when she can see again and takes your hand, understanding at that moment who you really are, that is when I loved you the most. It couldn't have worked if she'd heard your voice

DOUGLAS You're taking a tremendous risk, Charlie – a silent film in this new age of sound

CHARLIE It's not a silent film, Douglas. I've written music for it. It's just not a talkie

Piano plays.

SYDNEY Charlie...it's Ma

CHARLIE *moves towards* **SYDNEY** *and they grieve together.*

CHAPLIN On 28th August 1928, Hannah Chaplin died. I visited her
every day. You could see she was in pain. The day before she
died, we were laughing together. And then there was a release.
I suppose when life tortures, death is welcome. But then the
following day, seeing somebody beloved and small, you think
of all the events of life...all the battles she had fought

He cries.

And... I couldn't touch her... I couldn't

Shouting appreciative crowd.

Scene 18

DOUGLAS Boy you've done it! What a hit! There's been a line running round the block ever since ten this morning and it's stopping the traffic. They're fighting to get in and you should hear them yell!

Excerpt of that scene from City Lights may be shown but only if licensed by the **CHAPLIN** *office*.*

Loud cheers, tears and hope from chorus.

CHAPLIN *(to audience)* City Lights was released in 1931 at the beginning of the Great Depression, a period of distress and destitution when the figure of the hungry and dishevelled Tramp becomes more pertinent than ever before.

(to **CHARLIE***)* The people look to you for hope, Charlie

CHARLIE But I don't have much time left, do I?

CHAPLIN What?

CHARLIE If you're never going to let me speak

CHAPLIN I can't make films with all that stuff going on – cameras as big as elephants, massive sound boxes recording every little sneeze and burp, acres of wires and switches – how are you going to manoeuvre yourself around all that and be – you? There's no room for your park and your policeman and your pretty girl

PAULETTE GODDARD *joins* **CHARLIE**. *A sweetheart.*

CHARLIE Paulette Goddard. My new leading lady. She's twenty-two *(defensively)*

CHAPLIN And she's moved into your mansion

CHARLIE The kids just love her

PAULETTE I love them

CHARLIE Let us speak, please, let us speak in this film, this... Modern Times. It's modern times – for God's sake

CHAPLIN No. It's important that the Little Fellow remains an innocent. In the factory system that channels and standardizes men, you are two joyous spirits living by your wits. You will not be turned into machines

CHARLIE I get eaten by a machine!

CHAPLIN That proves my point

An excerpt from Modern Times *where* **CHARLIE** *is "eaten" by the machine may be shown but only if licensed by the* **CHAPLIN** *office*.*

CHARLIE *(to* **CHAPLIN***)* It's you isn't it. Me struggling with all the factory technology is you struggling with the new world of film. It's not that you won't. You can't!

CHAPLIN *Modern Times.* 1936. The Little Tramp becomes obsolete

Excerpt from film of **CHARLIE** *and* **PAULETTE** *making their way down a long and dusty road may be shown but only if licensed by the* **CHAPLIN** *office*.*

CHARLIE *and* **PAULETTE** *re-enact the moment when* **CHARLIE** *and* **PAULETTE** *prepare to walk down the long and dusty road.*

CHARLIE and **PAULETTE** Buck up. Never say die! We'll get along

They turn and go.

CHARLIE *and* **CHAPLIN** *part forever.*

CHAPLIN *Modern Times was* the Little Tramp's last film. Not entirely silent. I wrote the music of "Smile" for it.

And so it was.

All my films came from those words of my mother's

He sings "SMILE".

And is joined by all.

The End

Material sourced from:

My Autobiography – Charles Chaplin
Chaplin The Tramp's Odyssey – Simon Louvish
Chaplin His Life and Art – David Robinson
Charlie Chaplin Interviews Edited by Kevin J Hayes
Charlie Chaplin – John McCabe
Chaplin and American Culture – Charles J Maland
Chaplin Movie Icons – Taschen
Charlie Chaplin – Peter Ackroyd

Films clips from the following films are pre 1918 and in the public domain but if you use restored dvds, you should seek permission from the owners of the material on the dvd.

Kid Auto Races at Venice
Mabel's Strange Predicament
The Tramp
The Immigrant

Film clips from the following films should be licensed:

The Kid
The Gold Rush
City Lights
Modern Times

License from:

*Roy Export S.A.S.
58 rue Jean Jacques Rousseau
75001 Paris – France
Tel: +33 1 40 26 31 23
Fax: +33 1 42 36 42 90
Official site: www.charliechaplin.com
email: office@charliechaplin.com

PROPERTY LIST

Scene 1

Onstage: Rows of costumes and film-set paraphernalia. Long mirror. Sewing machine.   The Little Tramp's costume

Sofa and stools for the Chaplin's attic home. Various wooden boxes (eg Hannah's seat in the asylum/divorce court etc.)

Scene 4

Hannah: Large bag containing two pairs of clogs

Scene 5

Circus performers: Circus ribbons, other circus paraphernalia

Charlie: False moustache

Scene 7

Charlie: Violin

Scene 8

Guys and Gals: Leather suitcases

Charlie: Winged collar, rouge

A door. A ladder.

Charlie: The Little Tramp's costume

Scene 9

Sydney: Letter

Scene 10

Charlie and Sydney: Paintbrushes

Scene 11

Crowd: Drinks

Scene 13

Mildred/Charlie: Baby

Scene 14

Edna: Scarf

Scene 15

Charlie: Costumes, hats and canes for dance

Scene 16

Douglas, Mary and Charlie: Celebratory drinks

Charlie: Bread rolls on forks

LIGHTING PLOT

General lighting will cover the space for most of the scenes and will also fade in and out of different areas.

To open

Low lighting fades up on Charlie as he appears and dresses

Scene 1

Increase lighting to include Chaplin

Scene 2

Ta Ra! Ra! Boom De Ay!
Bright theatrical lighting on chorus

Chaplin moves to Charlie
Return to general lighting

Scene 3

Their attic room
Fade up on attic

Scene 4

Chaplin: Poor Hannah
Increase light to include asylum

Eight Lancashire Lads
Bright theatrical lighting on chorus

Scene 5

Circus scene
Bright theatrical lighting on circus performers

Scene 6

Charlie and Sydney go to see Hannah
Fade up on asylum

Scene 7

Warm general lighting

Scene 8

The guys and gals embark for America
Bright general lighting
Fade during film clips if used

Scene 9

Sydney reads letter
Fade up onto Sydney

Scene 10

Sydney: Can you put me up for the night?
Bright theatrical lighting
Scene 11

Charlie finds Edna Purviance in the café
Fade up on café

He takes her to a party
Fade up on party

Scene 12

Fade party lighting during film clips if used

Edna: I wanted to call him back
Return to general lighting
Fade during film clips if used

Scene 13

Change to warm lighting

Charlie holds the dead baby
Focus lighting on Charlie and Mildred

Scene 14

Vaudeville act
Bright theatrical lighting on singer and chorus
Change to general lighting

He turns to Edna
Fade to scene with Edna

Divorce court
Cross fade to divorce court

Back in scene
Return to general lighting
Fade during film clips if used

Scene 15

Lots of Charlie Chaplins appear
Bright theatrical lighting on chorus

Scene 16

General lighting
Fade during film clips if used

Scene 17

General lighting

Chorus and Al Jolson sing "My Mammy"
Bright theatrical lighting on singer and chorus

Charlie moves towards...
Focus light on Charlie and Sydney

Chaplin: On 28th August
Add focus light on Chaplin

Scene 18

General warm lighting
Fade during film clips if used

Chaplin sings "Smile"
Focus on Chaplin

And is joined by all
Bright theatrical lighting on all

EFFECTS LIST

Live pianist plays all except:

Clog Dance: Suggest **Nottingham Swing** – The Cheviot Ranters

Circus scene: Suggest **Knock Out Drops** – Sounds of the Circus South Shore Concert Band

Charlie Chaplins Dance: Suggest **The Reel Chaplin** – Carl Davis and the City of Prague Orchestra

Scene 8

The guys and gals embark for America; Ships horn

Lightning Source UK Ltd.
Milton Keynes UK
UKOW05f1145240916

283705UK00001B/22/P